ORTHODOX COLORING BOOK

WORLD'S FAMOUS ORTHODOX CHURCHES FOR COLORING

SIMON OSKOLNIY

ABOUT THE BOOK

Great for kids or adults, this book lets you color world's most famous Orthodox churches. From Church of the Savior on Spilled Blood in St. Petersburg to the Alexander Nevsky Cathedral in Bulgaria, this is a great way to reaffirm your connection with the Orthodox faith.

CONTENTS

This page intentionally left blank.

1. Church of the Savior on Spilled Blood

2. St. Basil's Cathedral

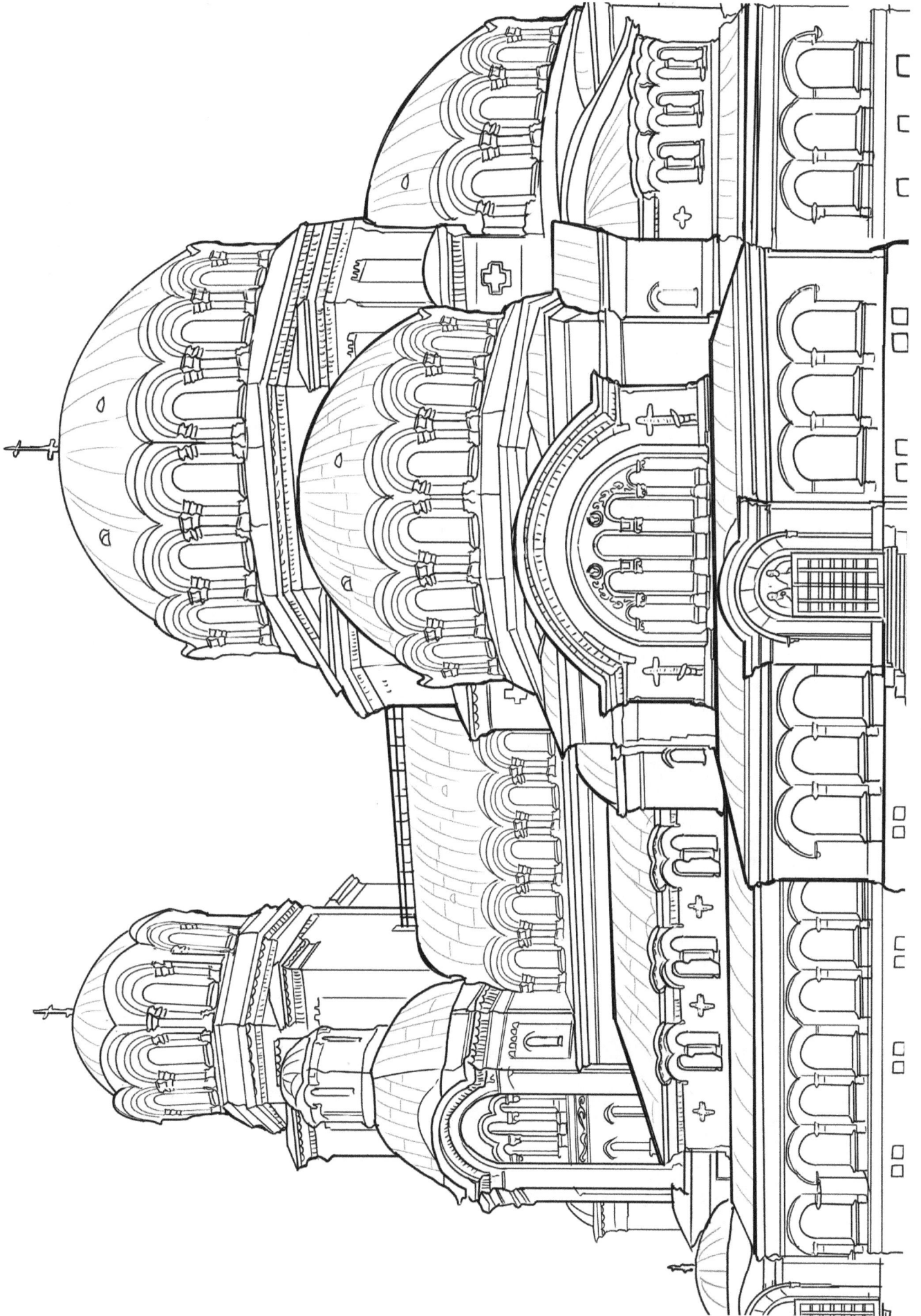

3. Alexander Nevsky Cathedral

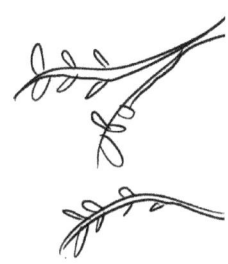

9

4. Smolny Cathedral

5. Belfry and Church of the Transfiguration

6. Cathedral of Christ the Saviour

7. St. Sophia Assumption Cathedral

8. St. Sophia Church

This page intentionally left blank.

ABOUT THE BOOK

Great for kids or adults, this book lets you color world's most famous Orthodox churches. From Church of the Savior on Spilled Blood in St. Petersburg to the Alexander Nevsky Cathedral in Bulgaria, this is a great way to reaffirm your connection with the Orthodox faith.